Aquaponics

How to Build your own Aquaponic Garden that will Grow Organic Vegetables

By Andrew Johnson

"The love of gardening,

Is a seed once sown

That never dies."

- Gertrude Jeckyll

Table of Contents

Introduction

Chapter 1: Aquaponics: Why it will get you hooked
   1.1 The many angles of aquaponics
   1.2 Plants love fish
   1.3 How does aquaponics differ?
   1.4 Why choose aquaponics?

Chapter 2: How aquaponics works: The symbiosis between fish, plant & bacteria
   2.1 The nitrogen cycle
   2.2 Bacteria are your friends

Chapter 3: Designing your aquaponic unit
   3.1 Basic aquaponic design
   3.2 Ideal growing conditions to consider
      Sunlight
      Temperature
      Protection from the elements
      Space
      Location
   3.3 The best systems for aquaponic gardening from home
      Flood and Drain Technique
      Nutrient Film Technique (NFT)
      Media Bed Technique
   3.4 System parts and materials
      Growing trays
      Types of growing media
      Cups and nets
      Pumps and fittings
      Air-pumps
   3.5 System design considerations
      Sediment filters
      Bio filters
      Sumps
   3.6 Sizing your system

- System ratios
- Calculating outputs
- Calculating inputs
- Fish populations
- Stocking density
- Bio filter size
- Water volume
- Variations and design considerations

Chapter 4: Essential elements – Things to know before you start
- 4.1 Water
- 4.2 Health and safety
- 4.3 Starting an aquaponic system

Chapter 5: Bacteria - Essential tiny creatures
- 5.1 Bacteria-friendly environments
- 5.2 Sourcing bacteria
- 5.3 System Cycling
- 5.3 Monitoring bacteria

Chapter 6: Casting a light on finding the correct fish
- 6.1 Selecting fish
- 6.2 Sourcing fish
- 6.3 Fish-friendly environments
- 6.4 Fish care
- 6.5 Monitoring fish

Chapter 7: Finding plants that love those fish
- 7.1 Selecting plants
- 7.2 Sourcing plants
- 7.3 Plant-friendly environments
- 7.4 Plant care

Chapter 8: System monitoring & maintenance
- 8.1 Water monitoring
- 8.2 System adjustments
- 8.3 Regular maintenance

Chapter 9: Reeling in the success – Optimizing your aquaponic system
- 9.1 Plant choices
- 9.2 Propagating your own plants
- 9.3 Staggered plantings and plant diversity
- 9.4 Fish polycultures
- 9.5 Supplementing fish feed

   9.6 Precautionary additions
   9.7 Planning for system changes
Chapter 10: Troubleshooting: Fixing your fishy business
   10.1 Plant health: Help, my plants are sick!
   10.2 Cleaning: Help, my growing environment is dirty!
   10.3 Fish: Help, my fish are unhappy!
   10.4 System measurements: Help, my system is unbalanced!
Chapter 11: Parting Words

Introduction

At the local community garden, I have a friend with a garden called "Fish and Chips and Salad". It is only a small garden, about 18 square feet (2m²), and it looks quite strange. In addition to the signage, half of the garden is taken up by a large tank.

It may be a little gimmicky, but the name of that garden reveals an inspiring goal: to raise all of the ingredients needed for the titular meal. In that tiny garden, my friend really is growing fish, and potatoes, and salad. And what makes the garden even more special is that the entire meal will be grown with no waste, and no external input. How? Through aquaponics.

The term "aquaponics" originated in Cold-War era America, where A-bomb fears led to the combination of aquaculture (raising fish for consumption) and hydroponics (soil-less plant production). Scientists realized that these growing systems, which combine plants, fish and bacteria in a symbiotic system, could successfully produce food in small spaces, or even underground, should the need arise.

However, the 1950s "preppers" were not the first to use aquaponics. In fact, it is an age-old growing system. The Ancient Khmer, who built Cambodia's Angkor Wat, introduced fish to their rice paddies in order to control insects and provide fertilizer, a practice still used throughout South East Asia today. A similar method of agriculture, where plants grow on floating structures and rely on the nutrients provided by aquatic life, has also been practiced by other ancient cultures including Mexico's Aztecs, Bolivia's Uru peoples and the Egyptians of the Nile Delta.

While a system which balances bacteria, plants and fish may sound complicated, aquaponics is surprisingly simple. It allows you to produce a whole meal in a compact, environmentally-sustainable unit, and to create a self-sustaining ecosystem on a home scale.

This book is intended as a starting point for creating a backyard aquaponic system. It outlines how aquaponics works and the nature of the symbiosis between the elements. It also includes a brief overview of the different types of aquaponics systems, and trouble-shoots some common problems faced by home growers.

It is a long-term goal, but imagine how amazing that first meal of fish, and chips, and salad will be when grown in your own aquaponics system. Bon appétit!

Chapter 1:

Aquaponics: Why it will get you hooked

At its most basic, aquaponics is nothing more than a plant grown in symbiosis (a mutually-beneficial relationship) with fish or other aquatic creatures. If you have a weeds or plants in your aquarium, you are practicing aquaponics.

1.1 The many angles of aquaponics

An aquaponics system is a closed-system permaculture with three components:

1. Fish

2. Plants

3. Bacteria

These three components live side-by-side and work together to create an environment that is mutually advantageous. This means that the correct balance of each is required for the system to be healthy and functional. Achieving this balance, the pursuit of which is a little addictive, is the main goal of the aquaponic grower.

1.2 Plants love fish

The needs of a plant are simple: air, water and nutrients. When provided with these essentials, plants then use the process of photosynthesis to convert ambient light into glucose, which is the building block of all vegetable matter.

Plants require a range of nutrients in different amounts in order to photosynthesize successfully. The beauty of aquaponics is that fish can provide plants with these nutrients. It is no wonder that plants love fish!

In a standard garden, animal manures might be used to provide plants with the nutrients that they need to grow. However, these manures must be composted or processed in order to make the nutrients they contain accessible.

In the same way, an aquaponic system functions when bacteria process fish waste, converting it into nitrates. This provides the plants with the nutrients they need to grow in a highly accessible form.

The aquaponics cycle begins when fish are fed, and create waste. This waste is largely ammonia, which can be fatal to fish at high levels. Therefore, nitrifying bacteria break it down into plant food. In absorbing this food, plants filter the water, which is then returned to the fish tank.

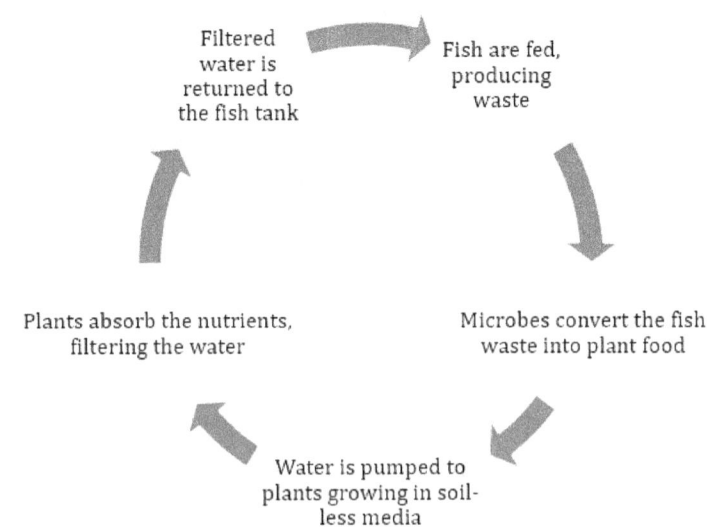

Figure 1: A basic aquaponics cycle

1.3 How does aquaponics differ?

Some people might thing hydroponic and aquaponic gardening are very similar, and in some regards there are similarities, but there are certainly significant differences between the two methods of gardening. Whereas the hydroponic garden is a garden without soil, the aquaponic garden focuses mainly on a symbiosis of nutrients between plants and fishes. Also, both systems are very different from regular gardening as well. In a regular garden, the needs of plants are generally provided for in a more natural way:

- Sun provides light
- Rain provides water and may be supplemented with irrigation
- Soil provides a growing media and the nutrients that plants require

Growers may also improve the soil and provide plants with additional nutrients using fertilizers and composts.

In a hydroponic garden, on the other hand, the growing environment is more controlled:

- Plants are grown in an inert media
- Water is constantly cycled past plant roots, providing hydration
- Nutrients are provided in the cycling water, and come from custom-made, chemical mixes

The advantages of hydroponics over regular gardens include the improved hydration, as well as the higher level of control that growers have over the nutrients available to plants. Nutrient solutions are customized to suit plant species and their stage in the growth cycle, leaving to more consistent yields and improved production overall.

In comparison with natural gardening, aquaponic systems are similar to hydroponics with one key difference:

- Nutrients in the cycle come from fish, which produce waste that is then converted into available plant food by bacteria

1.4 Why choose aquaponics?

While aquaponics is not as exact as hydroponics when providing for specific crop needs, it is more economical: Aquaponics does not require expensive chemical inputs, has less waste-water and provides the grower with two crops (fish and plants) from the same space and inputs.

Aquaponic systems are also highly adaptable, making them a suitable garden choice for a variety of different climates, locations, spaces and needs. The systems are surprisingly simple to set up. They can be small or large, located indoors or outside, and can successfully support any number of aquatic creatures and plant species.

Aquaponics also appeals to those concerned with health and food security. The fish and vegetables produced in the system are more reliable than those produced commercially, as aquaponics are naturally organic and the grower knows exactly what their produce has come into contact with. Additionally, oily fish such as carp and trout raised in an aquaponic system on a controlled died have higher levels of omega-3 fatty-acids, which have been linked to cancer-prevention and other health benefits, than fish from commercial sources.

Chapter 2:

How aquaponics works: The symbiosis between fish, plant & bacteria

It is important even for the hobby aquaponic gardener to have a good understanding of the basic biological processes which form the bonds between the components of an aquaponics system. Without these processes taking place in due course, the system will not work. But when the system is working, it has the potential to provide for a wide-range of needs in a variety of spaces and climates.

2.1 The nitrogen cycle

Nitrogen is the most important element in the formation of all organic matter and one of the most abundant elements in the atmosphere. However, plants, except those in the legume family, cannot absorb atmospheric nitrogen. Therefore, in order for plants to access the nitrogen that they need for growth, it must be made available in the soil. In the natural environment, the nitrogen used by plants was once organic matter which has been processed by animals and bacteria as part of the nitrogen cycle.

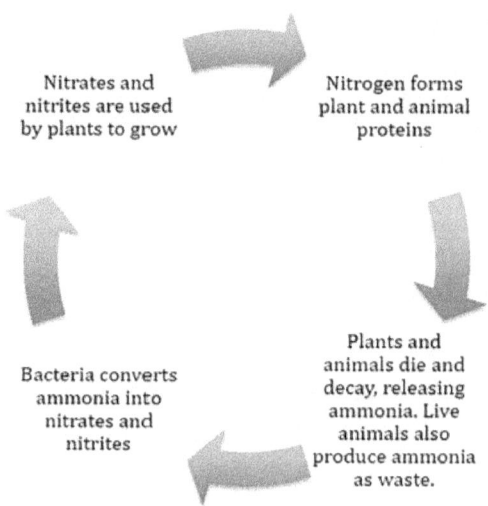

Figure 2: The nitrogen cycle The nitrogen in the soil usually begins as ammonia, produced as a waste product by decaying animal and vegetable matter, or as animal effluent. Ammonia can be processed by plants, but is not highly

accessible and often causes root-burn.

Fortunately there exists a group of bacteria known as "nitrifying" bacteria. These bacteria process ammonia, making it in to compounds which are more easily accessible to plants, such as nitrites and nitrates. It is these same compounds that make up many of the commercial fertilizers available from your local garden store. Without nitrifying bacteria, plants would not have the nitrogen that they need to grow and thrive.

2.2 Bacteria are your friends

Anyone who has ever kept an aquarium will know that fish are much more likely to die right after their tank has been cleaned. While stress plays a role, a more important factor is that the beneficial bacteria which process the fish waste have been "cleaned out" with the waste water. Even if you only replace part of the water, the remaining bacteria will still have to recolonize the tank, a process which may take days. If the recolonization is too slow to cope with the ammonia produced by the fish, they will perish.

It is clear, then, that nitrifying bacteria are absolutely vital for a healthy and functioning aquaponics system. Not only do they create the nutrients that help plants to thrive, they are absolutely vital for processing ammonia and maintaining fish health.

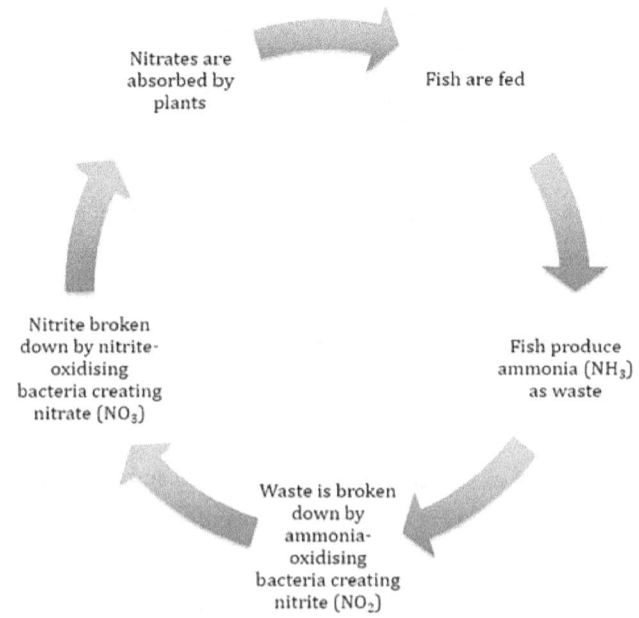

Figure 3: The nitrogen cycle in an aquaponics system In an aquaponic system, nitrifying bacteria may be present in the water, growing media and/or bio filter. As their role within the cycle is crucial for nutrient flow, make sure they are well taken care of and they love their living environment. Let's look at how we design this living environment in more detail in the next chapter.

Chapter 3:

Designing your aquaponic unit

There are many different types of aquaponic systems – this book covers just a few – and the system chosen will depend on your needs as well as the resources which you have available. There are many pre-fabricated units available for purchase, but it is also possible to construct your own. It all depends on budget and practical ability.

This chapter will give an indication of the environmental and practical factors to be considered when designing and locating an aquaponic system. Keep in mind that most growers will utilize elements from different systems in order to best meet their gardening needs.

3.1 Basic aquaponic design

Prior to considering the various system types, it is necessary to examine the basic design of an aquaponics unit. Generally speaking, units consist of two main components: a fish tank; and a grow bed for raising plants.

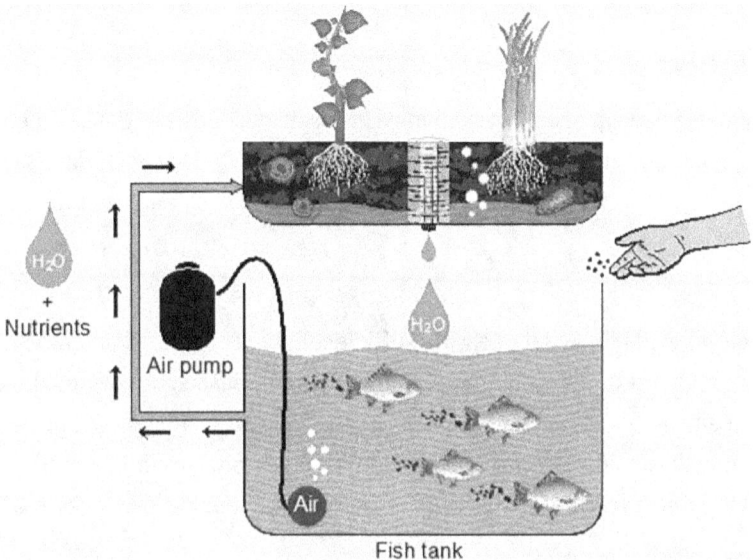

Figure 4: Basic aquaponic unit Some systems are more complex and may also include sumps or water reservoirs, bio-filters, sediment filters. And, of course, there are hundreds of different grow bed designs available to suit difference spaces and plant types.

3.2 Ideal growing conditions to consider

When situating a garden or a fish tank, we take the needs and preferences of our plants or animals into account. However, with an aquaponics system, growing conditions are doubly complicated as the needs of plants, fish, bacteria *and* their human guardians, must be taken into account.

Sunlight

The plants in an aquaponic system have the same needs as any others – between 2 and 6 hours of sunlight per day, depending on variety. However, the fish, bacteria and any exposed water in an aquaponic system should be protected from sunlight.

Therefore, while it is vital to ensure sufficient light for robust plant growth, as much of the rest of the system as possible should be shaded or covered. In the case of situating a system under cover or indoors, artificial lights can be utilized as with hydroponics. However, similar precautions as with sunlight need to be taken to protect fish and bacteria, and to prevent algae in exposed bodies of water.

Temperature

Although ambient temperature should also be considered, in particular with regard to maximum and minimum temperatures, realistically, it is water temperature which will be of most importance in an aquaponics system.

While plants are relatively hardy, fish and bacteria have very specific temperature requirements for optimum growth.

Fish are very susceptible to temperature fluctuations. It is for this reason that fish tanks should always be shaded and water temperature should be regularly monitored. Additionally, maximum and minimum temperatures need to be taken into account when choosing suitable fish varieties for your system. If possible, the system should be situated so that extreme fluctuations of temperature are unlikely.

The productivity of nitrifying bacteria is also affected by temperature. Although some processing will continue even at low temperatures, nitrification occurs most effectively between 60 and 85 degrees Fahrenheit (15-30°C) so in cool climates, systems will need protection from low temperatures.

Of course, because aquaponics runs on water, temperatures below freezing will not only affect the living creatures in the system, but also have the potential to damage pumps and pipes.

Protection from the elements

Although sunlight and temperature are the primary concerns to be taken into account when locating an aquaponic system, protection from the elements should also be considered:

- Wind can have an impact on water temperatures and evaporation, and taller plants may also require some shelter for optimum growth.

- Rainfall can alter pH and nutrient levels in a system, so it is usually recommended that systems have some cover.

Space

Aquaponic systems can be extremely compact if necessary, and are adaptable to all sorts of spaces. It is best to begin with a small system, and to allow yourself room to expand once you have perfected the system balance. The learning curve faced by the beginning grower can be steep, which becomes expensive in a massive system.

Location

An aquaponic system is much more complicated than a garden, and location can be the key to easy management. In choosing a location, in addition to the aforementioned considerations, you should also take into account that:

Aquaponic systems require daily monitoring

Choose somewhere convenient and accessible. If your unit is visible from your home, so much the better. Sometimes between 5 to around 10 minutes can be the difference between a loss of all of your fish, and their survival.

Electricity and water will be needed to run the system

Make sure you have running water and electricity present near your aquaponics growing location before starting to build your own aquaponic unit. Also save some space for the needed locations for extra waste and nutrient storage.

Systems should be secure

Systems can be a hazard to small children and animals, as there are exposed cords, pumps and bodies of water. Additionally, the plants and fish will require protection from predators, such as wild animals and domestic pets.

3.3 The best systems for aquaponic gardening from home

It is up to you to decide what type of aquaponic system best suits your needs as a gardener, as well as the space that you have available. All of the systems covered in this book are relatively easy to construct and function well on a home scale. The different systems have the same common elements, with different constructions or water cycles. This section considers the various systems available, including their strengths and uses, in order to help you make the choice that is right for you.

Flood and Drain Technique

Flood and Drain systems are a good starting point for the beginner and easy to manage on a home-scale. Plants are grown in a grow bed (or several) either situated directly above the fish tank, or connected to a drain. The grow bed is flooded with water which then drains back to the tank.

Flood and Drain systems require minimum pumping power and the growing media contained in the beds makes the use of a sump or bio filter, and the related additional pumps, unnecessary in most home applications.

On the other hand, these systems are larger than other options, as they require horizontal space for the grow beds. Additionally, if the drain cycle is reliant on a bell-siphon, as is most common, there can be the risk of malfunction, leading to the emptying of the fish tank unless an emergency shut-off valve is installed.

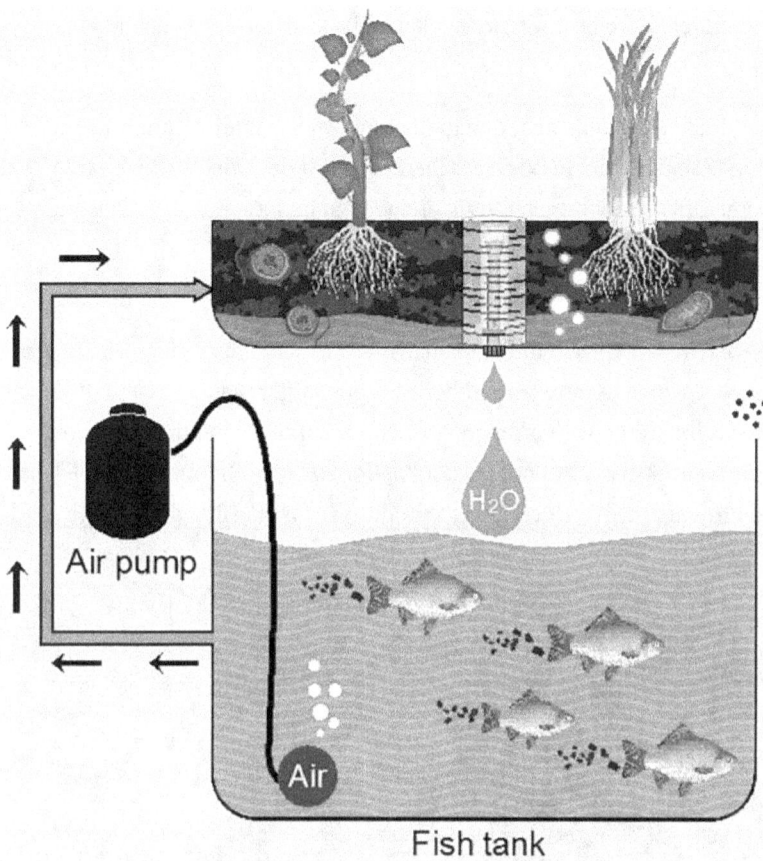

Figure 5: Flood and Drain Unit

Nutrient Film Technique (NFT)

Nutrient Film Technique (NFT) is one of the most common growing methods used in conjunction with aquaponics. Plants are grown in tubes through which low-volume water is passed. Round tubes are commonly used, but square-bottomed tubes are best for larger plants like tomatoes and cucumbers.

This method is reliable and, due to the low water volumes, monitoring and trouble-shooting tend to be easier than with systems which utilize large volumes of water. NFT grow beds are light and well-suited to vertical arrangements, making them perfect for small spaces.

NFT systems are better suited to smaller plants and those which easily grow water roots, such as lettuces and herbs. Some larger plants like tomatoes can be successfully grown with a support structure, but those requiring a larger, more supportive root-base will not be suitable for NFT. Additionally, as NFT has little or no growing media, it requires the addition of a bio filter and a particle filter.

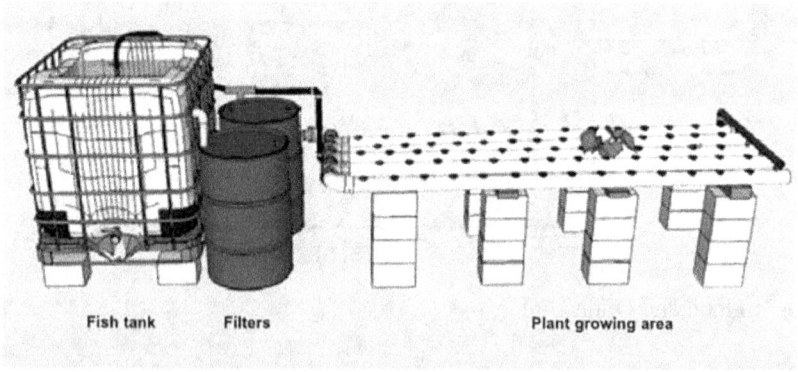

Figure 6: NFT Unit

Media Bed Technique

Media Bed Technique is similar to NFT in that water is flushed through or past plants using gravity, however, rather than growing tubes, plants are cultivated in grow beds containing growing media.

As with NFT, the low volume of water used in Media Beds is an advantage for monitoring and trouble-shooting. Additionally, Media Beds are well-suited to a greater variety of plants than NFT, because the growing media provides better root support. Growing media with good surface area can negate the need for a bio filter in smaller systems.

Like Flood and Drain systems, Media Beds require sturdy frames and horizontal arrangement, making them less space-saving than some other systems.

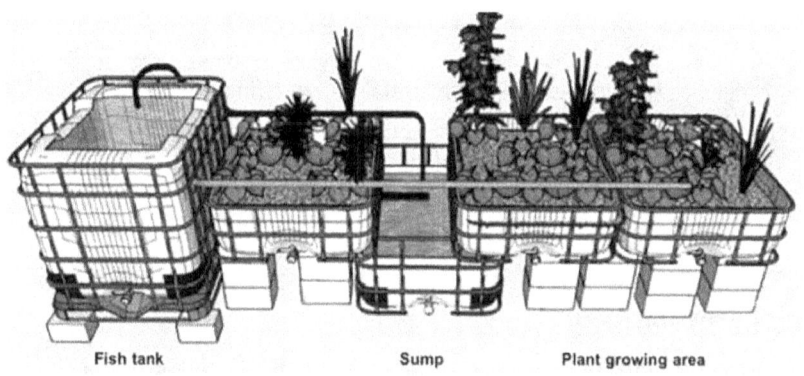

Figure 7: Media Bed System

3.4 System parts and materials

System parts which are common to most aquaponic units include the following elements.

Growing trays

Your growing tray is where the plants grow, so the size chosen will depend on how much you want to grow and the type of system you are using. Base the size and the depth of the tray on plant-growth predictions and recommended pot depths. Trays should be no less than 3 inches deep (15cm). For larger fruiting plants such as peppers and tomatoes, trays should be at least 6 inches deep (30cm).

Plastic or metal are the longest-lasting materials for growing trays, although Styrofoam is sometimes used. In most systems, trays need to be sturdy as they may hold large amounts of water and heavy growing media. They should always be opaque.

Types of growing media

Soil is not used in aquaponic systems because it is not sterile, compacts in contact with water, and tends to clog filters and pumps.

In an NFT system, plants are grown directly in water. In most other aquaponic set ups, a soil-less media is used. This growing medium, or substrate, is any material in which plant roots grow. There are many suitable growing media for use in aquaponics, but the main considerations are a media that does not degrade and contaminate the water, negatively affecting fish health, and one that has plenty of surface area in order to promote the growth of nitrifying bacteria.

Keep in mind that all growing media should be well-washed before use to remove dirt and particles. If in doubt about media quality, cycle water through the media and test for pH and hardness.

Stone wool

Also known as mineral wool, stone wool is a felt-like material manufactured from molten rock. In its raw form, stone wool has a very high pH but treated varieties designed for hydroponics (e.g. Rockwool) are suitable for aquaponic systems. Stone wool is used in NFT systems to provide additional root support for larger plants such as tomatoes and cucumbers.

Gravel and limestone

Gravel and limestone are some of the more inexpensive growing media and provide plants with good root support. Some rocks have a tendency to leach minerals, so testing should be conducted prior to use.

The downfall of these growing media is that they do not retain water very well, are exceptionally heavy and are abrasive to handle. They are not as conducive to the growth of bacteria as other options, due to a low surface area to volume ratio, making a bio filter necessary.

Pumice and volcanic gravel

These volcanic minerals are light and provide good root support. They are riddled with holes and air passages, like a sponge, so have a better surface area to volume ratio than actual rock, making them more conducive to bacterial growth.

Expanded clay beads

Expanded clay beads are a man-made equivalent to pumice and volcanic gravel. They are light, inert and retain water very well. They also have a very good surface area to volume ratio, encouraging beneficial bacterial. On the downside, clay beads are very expensive compared to other media, and can be slightly fragile.

Cups and nets

The growing tubes used in NFT systems are often fitted with cups or nets. Plastic cups and nets are small plant holders that look a little like a small pot with an extra-wide lip. Homemade cups can be made from Styrofoam, plastic or mesh, as long as there are plenty of holes big enough to allow root growth but not so big that growing media will escape into the nutrient solution.

Pumps and fittings

One or several pumps may be needed to cycle water in an aquaponic system. Most system designs utilize a pump for irrigating grow beds and gravity feeds for drainage. There is no "right" system design. It all depends on your needs.

Choosing a pump

There are many pumps available which are suitable for a backyard aquaponic unit. For a relatively small system, a water-feature (fountain) pump or pond pump is usually the most economical choice and will run on mains power. Your pump must be submersible and should have an in-built filter.

The size of pump you choose will depend on how far you need water to travel, and how much water you want to pump per hour. Stronger pumps are more expensive, but can be used to run more than one system if you have some plumbing expertise.

Pumps will list a pumping height and a maximum flow per hour. You should try to choose a pump which has a pumping height at least a foot (30cm) higher than your system requirements in order to ensure a good flow of water. Unfortunately, regardless of the stats given, maximum flow is not achieved at maximum pumping height, so allow for this in your calculations.

You also need to consider the amount of water you wish to pump per hour. Most systems require only low water volumes; as even small pumps have adjustable capacities of at least 30 gallons (100L), maximum capacity is not usually of concern except in very large systems.

Fittings and installation

Depending on the design of your system, you may require T-joins or drip irrigation fittings such as taps, perforated hose, micro-bubblers or end-plugs in order to ensure the even distribution of water in your growing tray. Note that water will not dispense evenly from more than one outlet unless the hose connecting the outlets is completely level, so care must be taken in construction.

Remember that pumps will burn-out if left to run dry. Check systems frequently and ensure that the pump NEVER has less than 4 inches (10cm) of head space (water above it).

Air-pumps

Depending on the size of your unit, you will also require several air-pumps. These usually take the form of some type of aquarium pump, and the more modern air-stones are particularly effective. Installing two pumps in your fish tank and another in your bio filter is usually good practice.

3.5 System design considerations

Although the numerous aquaponic system designs have shared elements, such as grow beds, fish tanks and pumps, there are also various features which can be fitted to systems as needed. Some key elements that might be included in the design of an aquaponic system are:

Sediment filters

Solid fish waste and uneaten food, as well as plant matter, will contaminate the water in an aquaponic system. Therefore, sediment filters, which remove solid waste, are a necessary part of most aquaponic units.

In Media Beds and Flood and Drain systems, growing media will act as a sediment filter, removing and storing any solid waste that passes through. However, using this method of sediment filtration alone can cause disease and lead to anaerobic conditions, inhibiting beneficial bacteria. At the very least, screens should also be used.

The simplest method of sediment filtration is fitting pipes, particularly those leaving fish tanks and grow beds, with a filter such as a mesh sieve or screen. Sediment will become trapped in the filter due to the pressure of passing water. This method requires the regular cleaning of the filter and is most suitable for small, lightly-stocked systems.

On a larger scale, water leaving the fish tank can be run through a particle filter made from a container filled with growing media or stone, and possibly some mesh screens or filter wool. These filters require less frequent cleaning than a screen or sieve, and do a more thorough job. Additionally, when the container is washed and flushed, the waste makes an excellent fertilizer for soil-grown plants.

On a larger scale, a mechanical filter might be needed, for example a swirl filter or a trickle filter. These components are widely available, and are included with many pre-fabricated aquaponic units. There are also numerous plans available for DIY options.

Bio filters

A bio filter is a tank intended to house the bacteria colonies that convert fish waste to nitrates. They are necessary in most of the larger aquaponic units and are a requirement of NFT systems in particular, as the lack of growing media means there are few other spaces for bacteria to colonize. Small systems with a low stocking density and grow beds using clay beads or volcanic stone may not require a bio filter.

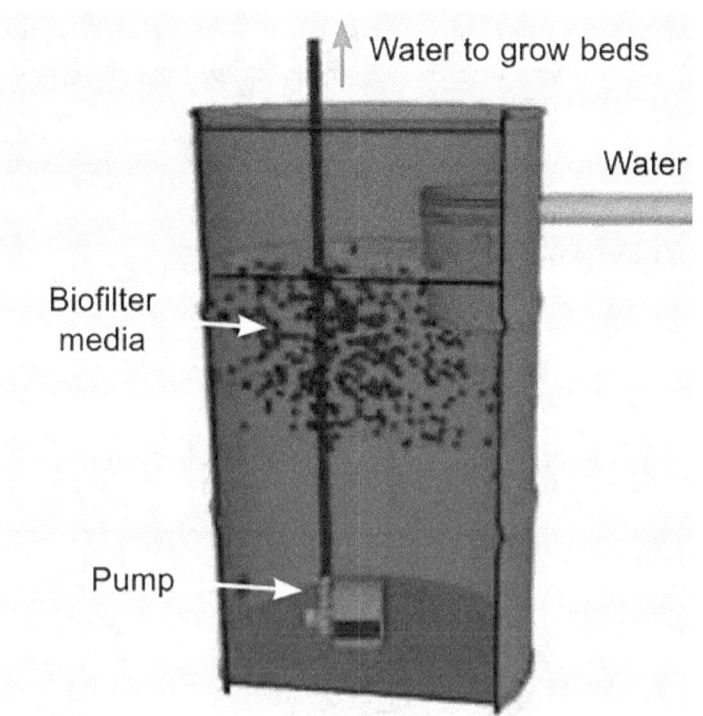

Figure 8: Example bio filter

Sumps

A sump essentially is a lower reservoir area which will collect the unwanted liquids from the aquaponic system. Although aquaponic systems are not reliant on a sump or water reservoir, a sump may take the place of a bio filter, depending on the system. Usually one of the two is used, or none at all. As with all containers of water, sumps should be opaque and covered. A sump is a useful component of an aquaponic system for several reasons: - It increases the overall volume of the system, providing for more beneficial bacteria. This also allows a greater time-lag between mechanical issues and the system running dry, thus protecting it.

- It provides greater freedom when arranging grow beds, as water can be directed to the sump as well as the fish tank.

- It allows for improved sediment filtration.

3.6 Sizing your system

Balancing the amount of fish, plants and bacteria in an aquaponic system is an absolutely essential process. Consider the results when one of these three components is out of balance: *Bacteria*

If not enough space is available for bacteria to colonize, colonies may be too small to process the amount of fish waste produced. Ammonia will accumulate in the system and cause fish deaths.

Fish

If there are not enough fish, plants will not receive sufficient nutrients to grow. Make sure you have a decent sized collection of fish.

Plants

If there are insufficient plants in the system, water will accumulate nutrients, in particular nitrates. Nitrate does not affect fish, but high concentrations can affect other elements of the ecosystem impacting fish health, such as pH and oxygen levels.

System ratios

The components of an aquaponic system are initially balanced by calculating the input and the output of the unit. That is, how many plants will be produced (output), and what amount of fish feed is needed each day to provide these plants with sufficient nutrition (input).

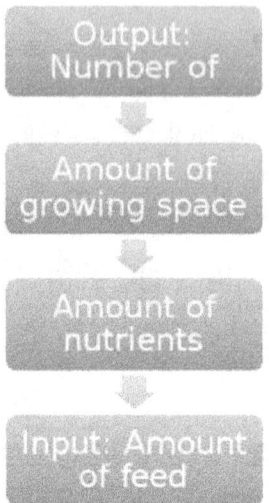

Figure 9: System input and output

Additional calculations include the number of fish needed to consume this feed, as well as the size of the bacteria colony needed to process the ammonia produced.

Figure 10: Fish stocks

Calculating outputs

Output is calculated in total square feet (or m²) of growing space. As in a standard garden, plant density in aquaponics will vary based on spacing recommendations for the chosen variety of vegetable and on the level of nutrients available. As a basic guide, leafy green herbs can be planted at a density of 2-3 per square foot (16-25 per m²). Fruiting plants require more space and may be planted at 1 per square foot or even less (4-8 per m²).

On a commercial level, outputs will be calculated down to the number of plants and will account for the time they take to reach harvest. However, on a home scale, where a range of vegetable plants will be produced for household use, an estimate of the growing space needed is a simpler approach.

Depending on your needs and the space you have available, an area of 6-18 square feet (2-6m²) of grow beds is usually a good starting point.

Calculating inputs

The amount of nitrogen needed, and therefore the input of fish feed in an aquaponic unit, is based on the nutritional needs of the plants being grown. As a rule, leafy green herbs require fewer nutrients than fruiting plants.

A general guide for inputs per day is:

- 0.2 oz. per square foot (40-50g per m²) of leafy green plants
- 0.3 oz. per square foot (50-80g per m²) of fruiting plants

In home units where a variety of different vegetable plants are grown, an estimate of the proportion of leafy greens to fruiting plants can be used to calculate the required system input.

Fish populations

After input has been calculated, it can be used to determine the number of fish needed to consume it. Fish populations are initially calculated as biomass (the total weight of the fish population), rather than in numbers, because a few large fish are likely to consume the same amount of food as many smaller ones.

If you intend to stock your tank with fingerlings, these fish will consume 10% of their body weight per day. Therefore, fish biomass for fingerlings can be calculated as follows: $\frac{\text{Input (oz. or g)}}{0.10} = \text{Fish biomass (oz. or g)}$

Juvenile and adult fish will consume 2% of their body weight per day. Therefore, fish biomass for juvenile or adult fish can be calculated as follows:
$\frac{\text{Input (oz. or g)}}{0.02} = \text{Fish biomass (oz. or g)}$

Once you have your biomass, you can calculate how many fish you need to populate your unit. Generally speaking, fingerlings weigh up to 1.7 oz. (50g), depending on species, while juvenile and adult fish will weigh 2-18 oz. (50-500g).

$\frac{\text{Fish biomass (oz. or g)}}{\text{Average fish weight (oz. or g)}} = \text{Number of fish}$

Species-specific and environmental factors will also influence the overall feed consumption and nutrient production of a fish population. However, on a home scale, variations are generally small enough as to be insignificant. Should you encounter problems, other factors that may also influence input and fish population include: - Water temperature (some fish eat less below a certain temperature)

- Fish species habits, including whether fish are carnivorous or omnivorous
- Feed quality and protein levels

Stocking density

Stocking density is also of importance to system function and fish health. A stocking density no higher than 44 pounds per 160 gallons (20kg per 1000L) is recommended.

Keep in mind that the higher the stocking density, the more quickly fish will suffer in the case of a pump or system malfunction, and the more aeration the fish tank will need.

Unless additional fish tanks are available or ongoing harvest in intended, the mature weight of fish should be used to calculate stocking densities, allowing for a fatality rate of 5-10%.

Bio filter size

Bio filters cannot really be too big, as the larger the size the more resilient the system will be to low temperatures, as well as fluctuations in ammonia levels and pH.

Bio filter capacity is based on available surface area, which determines the space that the nitrifying bacteria can colonize. It is for this reason that bio filters are filled with porous media (see Chapter 5).

In a home system bio filter size is usually determined by the containers available. As a general rule, 7 gallons of growing media or 3.5 gallons of bio filter are required to house sufficient bacteria to process one ounce of feed per day (1g of feed per 1L of growing media or 500ml of bio filter).

Water volume

The total water volume in an aquaponic system will not significantly impact on system ratios. The biological components are what is important.

Variations and design considerations

Like all elements of aquaponics, there will be variation to system ratios due environmental factors. Each system is slightly different and calculations are merely a guide for the beginning grower. Design your system based on the guide until you gain more experience, as ignoring system ratios usually leads to system destruction and fish death.

However, do not hesitate to make changes as needed based on regular water testing. If your system is consistently out of balance, there may be an issue with system ratios despite following the recommendations. Adjust as necessary, for example by increasing the size of the bio filter, or decreasing fish stocks.

Output: Number of plants	Input: Amount of feed	Fish populations
2-3 leafy green herbs per foot < 1 fruiting plant per foot	0.2 oz. per square foot of leafy greens 0.3 oz. per square foot of fruiting plants	For juvenile and adult fish: *Input ÷ 0.02 = Fish biomass* For fingerlings: *Input ÷ 0.10 = Fish biomass* Number of fish: *Fish biomass ÷ Average fish weight = Number of fish*

Stocking density	Biofilter size
Tanks > 130 gallons <44lb fish per 160 gallons	Media bed: 7 gallons per ounce of input Biofilter: 3.5 gallons per ounce of input

Figure 11: System ratio summary

Chapter 4:

Essential elements – Things to know before you start

While every system is different, and different plants and fish will have individual requirements, there are many concerns which are common to all aquaponic set-ups. This chapter gives an over-view of the things that you need to know before you begin to build your aquaponic system.

4.1 Water

Water is the life-blood of the aquaponics system. It provides the connection between fish, plants and bacteria, and it is water quality, first and foremost, which will impact of the health and functionality of the system. Although the three components of the system have slightly different preferences, water purity is a need shared by all.

Water sources

Water quality is absolutely vital for both fish and plant health. Rainwater is ideal for aquaponic systems, as it is the purest water available. However, it is necessary to test even rainwater, as many parts of the world suffer from mild acid rains and pollution.

Water from all other sources should be extensively tested, and treated as necessary, before use in an aquaponic system. Water from mains systems tends to be chemically treated, whereas water from aquifers and bores can have high levels of dissolved salts and minerals.

Common chemicals found in mains (tap) water

The majority of tap water in the Western World is chlorinated to kill bacteria and pathogens, which may be harmful to humans. However, chlorine is not just toxic to bacteria, but also to fish and many plants. If you plan to use chlorinated water in an aquaponic system, it must be treated first. Chlorine dissipates in contact with air, so by storing tap water in an open container for at least 48 hours, you can ensure that it will not harm your ecosystem. Chlorine will dissipate more quickly if the water is aerated.

Another common disinfectant used in drinking water is chloramine. Chloramine is not as easy to remove as chlorine, and if it is used in your area, you will need to invest in sodium metabisulfite tablets or an active carbon water filter.

Some countries use alternative disinfectants to treat drinking water, and it is important to find out what is used in your area and how to treat it prior to beginning your venture into aquaponics.

Water hardness and salinity

In addition to disinfectants, water contains any number of other minerals and chemicals. These may come from the water source, such as the rock of an aquifer, or be the result of further chemical treatments. It is for this reason that it is so important to test your water source thoroughly before use, and consult an expert to deal with any significant impurities. Salinity is of particular concern, and water with high salinity should be avoided in standard aquaponic units.

Water that stops soap from lathering or leaves a scale of lime is often referred to as "hard water". Hard water has two main causes, both of which stem from the rock that the water has had contact with. Hard water may have high levels of calcium, or high levels of carbonates. Although it is necessary to consider the mineral content of your water source, hard water can usually be used without harm to the organisms in an aquaponic system.

pH levels

pH is the measure of acidity or alkalinity of a solution. While bacteria, plants and fish all have slightly different pH preferences, generally speaking it is best to keep an aquaponic system in the neutral to slightly acidic range, with a pH of 6-7.5.

Microbial and fish activity can affect pH levels, as can certain growing media. The pH of a system will often decrease over time, requiring adjustment, but major changes are indicative of problems. Therefore, testing the pH of your water source and of the system itself is good practice to avoid instabilities affecting organism health.

4.2 Health and safety

As with any undertaking, aquaponic units do have several health and safety considerations which growers need to be aware of.

Using ammonia and other chemicals safely

Ammonia is highly toxic and should be stored safely at all times. It should not be inhaled, ingested or come into contact with the skin. Use of gloves, goggles and a facemask is recommended. If contact with skin occurs, wash thoroughly with plenty of water and soap. Contact a doctor or poisons information center immediately if ingested or inhaled.

Acids, bases and other chemicals used in the monitoring and adjustment of an aquaponic system pose similar risks to ammonia and should be treated similarly.

Using growing media safely

All growing media is potentially harmful. It is important to wear a facemask when dry-handling, as inhaled particles can cause lung disease. Stone wool is particularly harmful, containing particles similar to fiberglass.

Safety precautions for system handling

The largest hazard posed by an aquaponic system is electrical safety. Ensure your electricity source is grounded, and all cords are secured. Use drip loops where appropriate and never hang wires over water.

Wash your hands well with soap and water after handling system components.

The water contained in the system has the potential to cause skin irritation, in particular if pH or nutrient levels are outside of the recommended range such as in the initial stages of system cycling. Aquaponic water could cause severe illness if ingested.

Hygiene

In order to avoid introducing potentially harmful pathogens, which may affect system health as well as the security of the produce, strict hygiene procedures should be followed.

Hands and equipment should be washed thoroughly prior to working with the system. All materials introduced to the system, such as plants, animals and feeds, should be from a reputable, disease-free source. Any materials of dubious origin, such as seedlings raised in soil, should be sterilized prior to introduction. Gloves should be worn when handling fish. The system should be protected from potential contaminates such as birds.

Due to the nature of the system, it is absolutely vital that contaminants such as blood and bodily fluids do not come into contact with it. This includes feces and manures, despite their safe use in other forms of agriculture.

Healthy produce

As with any produce, that grown in an aquaponic system can carry potentially harmful pathogens. Risk is negated by preventing produce from coming into contact with the water, and by washing it thoroughly before consumption.

When consuming fish, never consume any which show signs or symptoms of disease. Do not consume fish raised in contaminated water, and purge live fish feed before use. Purge fish in a light salt bath for 2-3 days before slaughter.

4.3 Starting an aquaponic system

Starting an aquaponic unit is not so simple as building a system and adding fish and plants. Realistically, you may have a functioning system for months before it is ready to populate. It is vital that you undertake system cycling, which is the process of building a bacteria colony in an aquaponic unit, prior to adding fish, or even plants, to a system.

Ignoring this step in the process of setting-up your unit will result in the costly deaths of fish and plants. Don't even think about fish until you have your ammonia levels under control and you have significant levels of nitrates in your system.

Chapter 5:

Bacteria - Essential tiny creatures

Aquaponics relies heavily of the work of bacteria in order to prevent fish waste from reaching toxic levels. Bacteria therefore forms a vital link between the components of the aquaponic ecosystem, making it possible for plants to effectively filter water in the system.

There are three main groups of bacteria which are necessary for the functioning of an aquaponic system, and which are often referred to as the "bio filter":

1, Ammonia-oxidizing bacteria, converting toxic ammonia into nitrites;

2. Nitrite-oxidizing bacteria, which convert nitrites into nitrates, the most available form of nutrients for plants;

3. Heterotrophic bacteria, which break down solid fish and plant wastes into available micro-nutrients, which are also necessary for plant growth.

Although all three groups of bacteria are vital for the functioning of an aquaponic system, the main focus is the bacteria which deal with ammonia and nitrogen. The ammonia-oxidizing and nitrite-oxidizing bacteria are referred to together as nitrifying bacteria, and are the difference between the life and death of an aquaponic system. Without these bacteria, systems will quickly become toxic, resulting in mass fish deaths.

Additionally, healthy colonies of nitrifying and heterotrophic bacteria prevent the growth of less beneficial bacteria, which may infect plants or fish, and cause harm to the system, upsetting the vital balance of the system components.

5.1 Bacteria-friendly environments

It is very important to create an environment in your aquaponic system which is bacteria-friendly and will encourage the growth of a healthy bacterial colony. This encourages nitrifying and heterotrophic bacteria, which have similar environmental requirements, to reproduce in the system.

Environmental requirements

Both nitrifying and heterotrophic bacteria require the following elements.

A water temperature of between 60-85°F (15-30°C) Bacteria will survive at temperatures outside of this range, but their reproduction and productivity decreases. Therefore, it is particularly important to monitor ammonia levels in the colder months, even in established aquaponic units, as it is not uncommon for low temperatures to inhibit bacterial activity, resulting in system toxicity.

A water pH of 6-7.5

Not too high or low, otherwise your living environment will not be pleasant for the bacteria, plants and fishes.

Protection from sunlight

Nitrifying bacteria is photosensitive, so protection from UV light is important. Media beds offer natural protection, but care needs to be taken in systems that incorporate a bio filter to ensure that it is well-shaded. Additionally, sunlight leads to increased algae growth, which can inhibit bacterial function as well as clogging system components.

High oxygen levels

High levels of oxygen are required for nitrifying bacteria to thrive. Fortunately, fish and plants also prefer a well-oxygenated environment.

An additional advantage of providing an oxygen-rich environment is that it is disliked by the majority of unwanted bacteria which might otherwise colonize an aquaponic system, such as denitrifying bacteria and sulphate-reducing bacteria, both of which can create system conditions toxic to fish. Ensuring your system is rich in dissolved oxygen is one of the most reliable ways that you can ensure you are cultivating the right bacteria, not the unwanted kinds.

Bio filter requirements

A bio filter is a large tank which is intended to house the nitrifying bacteria in an aquaponic unit (heterotrophic bacteria will naturally colonize any areas where solid waste is found, such as the bottom of fish tanks, filters and grow beds). It is a requirement of NFT systems, and is a useful addition to most aquaponic units.

The benefits of a bio filter are twofold: it provides a suitable habitat for nitrifying bacteria, allowing larger colonies than are possible solely in grow beds, thus making ammonia poisoning more unlikely; and it allows for extra water in the system, protecting fish and bacteria in the case of a plumbing malfunction.

A bio filter should provide the ideal habitat for nitrifying bacteria, so must be opaque and covered, in order to protect bacteria from sunlight. Bio filters should also be well-aerated, and it is not uncommon to situate an air-stone within.

Nitrifying bacteria will grow on any wet surface, so the primary purpose of a bio filter is to provide a large amount of surface area for the bacteria to colonize. This might comprise a tank filled with one of the aforementioned growing media (porous volcanic stone or expanded clay beads work particularly well), with weighted plastic or Styrofoam packing beads (large enough not to clog filters or enter the system), commercially produced "Bio-filter Balls" or even with bundles of a large-gauge plastic fencing or net material. Any material which provides space for bacteria colonies to grow will work.

5.2 Sourcing bacteria

Heterotrophic bacteria exist naturally everywhere and will populate a new aquaponic unit in sufficient numbers that sourcing them is unnecessary.

Nitrifying bacteria also exist naturally in water and air, and will colonize a new aquaponic unit unassisted once system cycling is begun. However, many new aquaponic growers source nitrifying bacteria externally. Keep in mind that bacteria colonies are not made, they grow. Therefore, sourcing nitrifying bacteria externally merely hastens the process of system cycling somewhat, it does not negate it.

Nitrifying bacteria can be sourced in two ways:

1. Aquaponic, aquaculture and aquarium stores sell various "liquid" forms of nitrifying bacteria.

2. Water or bio filter material from a mature and balanced aquaponic system, or even an aquarium, can be used as a source of nitrifying bacteria.

Of these options, bottled bacteria can help to establish a bio filter more rapidly, but is expensive and can be difficult to source. If it can be ascertained that material from an established system is disease free, this is the best way to start system cycling. However, relying on natural and unassisted colonization is equally effective in the long term.

5.3 System Cycling

System cycling is the process of establishing a colony of nitrifying bacteria in an aquaponic unit. Even if bacteria is sourced from an aquaponics store or existing system, cycling will still be necessary in order to allow bacteria to colonize the new system in sufficient numbers to support fish.

Nitrifying bacteria reproduce relatively slowly, and therefore the process of system cycling can take anywhere between 2 weeks and 2 months, depending on the initial source of bacteria and environmental conditions such as temperature. Many beginning aquaponic growers become impatient, adding fish before the system cycling is complete. As there is insufficient nitrifying bacteria to process all of their waste, these fish will likely die and those that survive will be sickly and stunted from their prolonged exposure to high levels of ammonia and nitrite.

System cycling consists of gradually adding ammonia to a new aquaponic unit. The system is run, or the water cycled, as if the unit was complete and producing, even though there are no plants or fish. The addition of ammonia provides a food source for the nitrifying bacteria and encourages the establishment of a bio filter colony.

Sources of ammonia for system cycling

Various sources of ammonia can be used for system cycling. Options include the following.

Pure ammonia

In some countries, it is possible to purchase ammonia at hardwares or chemists.

Ammonia may also be available as a cleaner and can be used to system cycle provided it does not contain colorants, scents or other additives.

Fish food

Fresh fish food ground to a fine powder is an inexpensive ammonia source for cycling.

Biological sources

Animal manures and aged urine can be used as an ammonia source, but should be sterilized to ensure that unwanted bacteria and pathogens are not introduced to the system.

Fish

Fish stocked at an extremely low density – 1-2 per 9 cubic feet (1-2 per m³) – can be used as an initial source of ammonia. Aquarium feeder fish (stocked at 5-10 per 9 cubic feet (5-10 per m³) due to their tiny size) are usually the best choice as fatalities are high and these fish are unlikely to ever thrive. However, this source makes it very difficult to control ammonia levels in the system and is not recommended.

How to system cycle

Once the aquaponic unit is running and water flow is established, a small amount of ammonia is added to the system each day. This ammonia provides a constant food source for the nitrifying bacteria and encourages reproduction and the establishment of colonies.

When adding ammonia initially, the goal is to establish and maintain a system-wide ammonia level of less than a two hundredth of a percent (0.005%). Levels significantly higher than this will be toxic even to nitrifying bacteria and require the immediate dilution of water in the system.

Note that even pure ammonia is available in different strengths, so the amount added to the system will depend on the water volume of your unit as well as the concentration of your ammonia source. The following equation can be used to calculate the amount of ammonia to be added daily:

$$\text{Amount of ammonia solution needed} = \frac{\text{System volume} \times 0.005}{\text{Concentration of ammonia source (as decimal)}}$$

In a cycling system, ammonia-oxidizing bacteria will colonize the bio filter in the first week, causing an increase of nitrites in the water. After another week or so, the system will show both nitrites and nitrates, as colonies of nitrite-oxidizing bacteria become established.

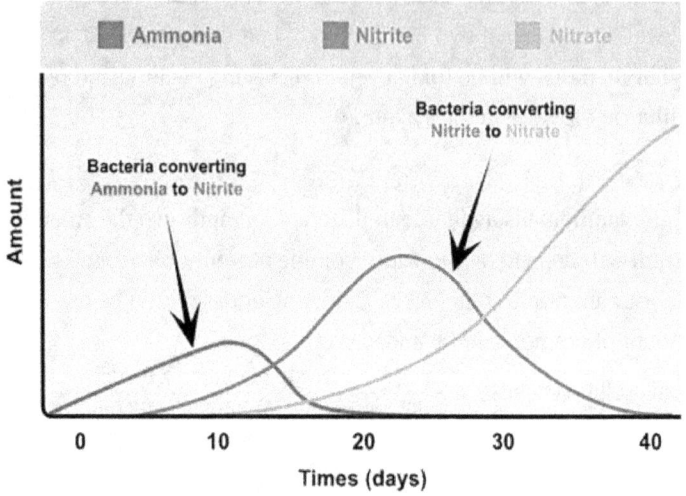

Figure 12: Successful system cycling

When the system has ammonia and nitrite levels of less than 0.00005 ounces per quart (1-2 mg per liter) – essentially, ammonia levels so low as to be immeasurable – the system cycling process is complete. Bacteria colonies are established and the system is ready for the addition of plants and fish.

Adding plants and fish

Although they are unlikely to thrive, plants can be added to an aquaponic system prior to the end of system cycling. Fish, on the other hand, should only be added once cycling is complete.

If you have completed the system cycling process but are not yet ready to add fish, a stable level of ammonia should be added to the system daily as when cycling. If this is neglected, your painstakingly cultivated bacteria colonies will quickly starve to death and you will have to begin the process again.

Fish should be added gradually to a new aquaponic unit, a couple at a time. Even in small numbers, fish are likely to produce more ammonia than the bacteria colonies are accustomed to processing. It will take the system a few days to reestablish an equilibrium and bring ammonia and nitrite levels back to below 0.00005 ounces per quarter (1mg per liter) once of fish that have been added.

5.3 Monitoring bacteria

Although a brownish slime in the bio filter or on other system surfaces is indicative of nitrifying bacteria, it is impossible to actually measure the population of the colonies successfully on a home scale. Instead, bacteria are monitored through measurements of ammonia, nitrites and nitrates.

Nitrites and nitrates will only be present in an aquaponic system through the functioning of nitrifying bacteria, and if a stable ammonia and nitrite level of below 0.00005 ounces per quart (1mg per liter) is maintained, it can be safely assumed that the bacteria in your system is healthy and happy.

Chapter 6:

Casting a light on finding the correct fish

A wide range of fresh water fish species are suitable for aquaponic use. The variety of fish that you choose will depend on the size of your system as well as environmental conditions, maximum and minimum temperatures being of particular importance. Additionally, many countries have strict regulations about which breeds of fish may be used in aquaculture in order to prevent the introduction of exotic species to local waterways.

6.1 Selecting fish

Some breeds of fish which are well-suited to aquaponic systems include the following.

Tilapia

Tilapia are one of the most popular fish for aquaculture due to their extreme hardiness and quick growth. They tolerate stress very well, are disease-resistant and thrive in aquaponic conditions, reaching their mature size in as little as 6 months. As omnivores, fish feed pellets can be partially replaced by cheaper plant foods.

Tilapia can be aggressive and cannibalistic. Additionally, they are very intolerant of cold water; while they will survive temperatures as low as 57 degrees Fahrenheit (14°C) they do not feed or grow outside of their ideal range of 68-86 degrees (20-30 °C), requiring heated water in colder climates.

Carp

Several carp species are used in aquaponic systems. Like tilapia, these fish are very tolerant of aquaponic conditions. They also have a much wider temperature tolerance, between 39 and 93 degrees Fahrenheit (4-34 °C), making them a better choice for both very hot and cold climates. Some carp are omnivorous, and they are well-suited to polyculture. Carp grow more slowly than tilapia, reaching maturity in 10-12 months.

Catfish

Catfish are another popular fish particularly well-suited to the beginning grower. They are resistant to many diseases and particularly tolerant of fluctuations in water quality, ammonia levels and pH. Some catfish are able to breathe air, and thus will not die if water ceases to flow or the air-pump stops. Catfish thrive in densely stocked aquaponic conditions and are suitable for polyculture. Catfish prefer water temperatures above 68 degrees Fahrenheit (20 °C).

Trout

Trout prefer colder temperatures than other fish, and thrive between 59-68 degrees Fahrenheit (15-20 °C), making them a good choice for temperate climates. They are a particularly popular choice for small, backyard aquaponic units for two reasons:

1. They are an oily fish rich in omega-3s, making them good choice for consumption.

2. On the same rations, trout produce more ammonia than other species, thus making it possible to support more plants with fewer fish.

Trout require a high protein diet, which can be costly to maintain if not supplemented with home-grown insects or worms. Fish will prey on each other if overstocked. Additionally, trout are much less tolerant of high stocking density, low oxygen levels, poor water quality or high ammonia levels, than the other fish previously mentioned.

Other options

Other species of edible fish successfully used in aquaponics include murray cod, perch, some species of bass and barramundi. Fish not suitable for consumption, such as koi, feeder fish and gold fish, can be used as well.

6.2 Sourcing fish

Fish for an aquaponic system can be sourced from aquarium or aquaculture suppliers. Fish purchased from aquaculture suppliers tend to be more economical than those from aquariums, and there are often discounts for bulk purchases. Remember when purchasing that you will not be putting the maximum stocking density into a new unit at once, and that as fish grow, density will increase. If buying in bulk, an additional holding tank with a filter and air-stone may be necessary.

Fish are available at a range of life-stages from tiny fry to mature adults. Fry are too small for aquaponic use. Fingerlings are suitable and cheaper to purchase, but require more care. Juvenile fish are hardier and more likely to tolerate system fluctuations, making them best suited to aquaponic use. They tend to reach a harvestable size after 6 months to a year in an aquaponic system.

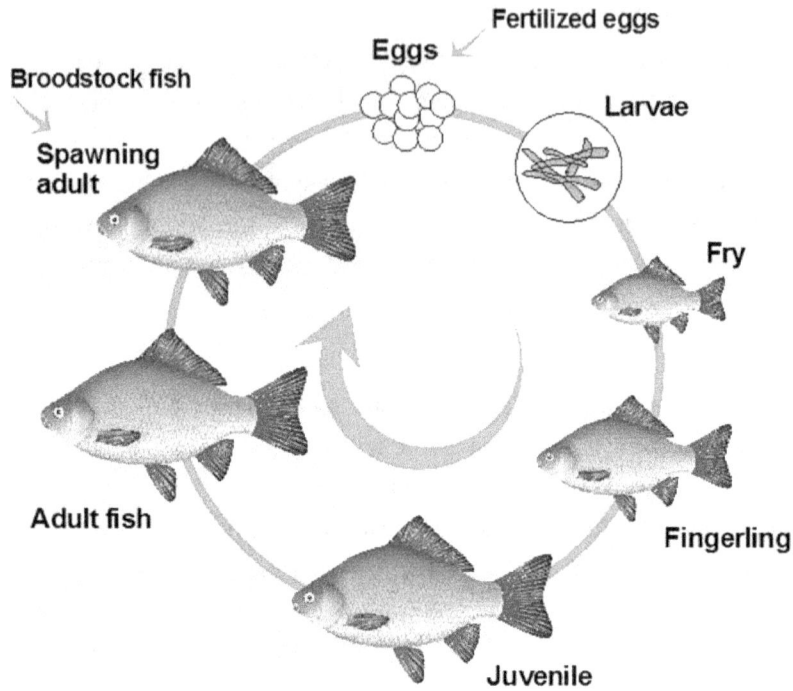

Figure 13: Fish life cycle

It is possible to breed new stock for your aquaponic system from mature fish. However, brood stock must be kept separately from the main system to reproduce. Tilapia can be bred fairly easily on a home-scale, whereas most other species of fish are difficult to breed.

As a beginning aquaponic grower, it is best to buy fish from a reputable supplier. Purchased fish are disease-free and more likely to tolerate the fluctuations in pH, ammonia levels and temperature common to a new aquaponic unit. Once you have a seasoned aquaponic unit and some experience with raising fish to maturity successfully, then you can think about raising your own fish.

It is important to note that in almost all countries, the poaching of fish from local water sources is illegal. These fish may not be suited to the conditions of an aquaponic system; they have the potential to introduce disease and may not be fit for consumption. Using caught fish is not recommended.

6.3 Fish-friendly environments

Different fish species have slightly different environmental requirements, and it is important to learn what these are and ensure that they are met. However, there are some general considerations to take into account.

Environmental requirements

Most fish species used in aquaponics require the following environmental elements to be present in order to be able to feel happy in their living environment.

Levels of ammonia & nitrite less than 0.00005 ounces per quart (1mg/l)

This keeps the water clean and healthy and avoids any type of poisoning or discomforting in the fish.

A stable pH

While different species of fish have different preferred pH levels, there are very few which tolerate large fluctuations. In fact, rapid pH changes can cause fatality.

Protection from direct light

Although fish prefer to have some, low-level light, protection from direct sunlight is necessary in order to prevent algae-growth and temperature fluctuations.

High oxygen levels

High levels of dissolved oxygen in the water are required for fish to breathe. Ensure that water is aerated (two air-stones or pumps for every 9 cubic feet (1m³) of water) and that fish are not overstocked. Discourage algae growth and remove sediment from the water, as these can both consume oxygen.

Protection from predation

Fish suffer from stress and need protection from predators such as wild animals, birds and domestic pets. Additionally, large fish of most breeds will prey on smaller fish; do not mix fish of different ages, or with large variations in size.

Fish tanks

Any opaque or translucent container can make an acceptable fish tank. Choose a tank which is large enough to allow you to expand your system to include more grow beds once it is fully stocked – at least 9 cubic feet (1m³). Fish tanks should not be less than 130 gallons (500L).

Ensure your fish tank allows a little light, and that covers are not air-tight, allowing oxygen to contact the water surface. Water pipes should be screened to prevent fish becoming trapped. Fish tanks should have at least one air-pump and two is recommended.

Stocking densities

Stocking density is important for fish health, as it impacts on environmental factors as well as fish stress levels. In a small-scale aquaponic system, a lower stocking density is recommended as filtration and oxygenation systems are less powerful than those used commercially. No more than 20 adult fish per 160 gallons (1000 liters) of total water is recommended.

6.4 Fish care

If you maintain system health and cleanliness, which is important for all three elements of an aquaponics unit, fish themselves will need minimal specific care. The most important thing you will have to do is feed them!

Moving fish

When introducing fish to a new environment, sudden changes to elements such as pH and water temperature can cause death. Whether you are adding new fish to you unit, or moving fish from one tank to another, introduce changes slowly.

Test both the fish's current environment and the destination. Then gradually alter conditions in the holding tank or container over 24-48 hours until they are the same as the destination. Changes can usually be achieved by slowly replacing the water in the holding tank with water from the destination. Once the environment of both places is the same, fish can be moved to the new location.

Particular care needs to be taken when placing new fish into an already stocked aquaponic unit. Place fish in a holding tank for 5-7 days if possible, monitoring closely for signs of disease, before introducing them to your system. Follow the procedure outlined above for introducing environmental changes.

Choosing a feed

Fish have particular dietary requirements for health and optimum growth. These requirements include a range of vitamins and minerals, as well as the correct proportions of proteins, fats and carbohydrates. Requirements vary throughout their life cycle, with growing fish requiring more protein than adult fish.

The easiest feeding option for home aquaponics is to purchase a pelletized fish food. It is possible to make homemade feed, but it's unlikely to meet all the needs of growing fish. Most commercial fish food, on the other hand, is a "complete" feed, meaning that it contains all of the elements that fish need to grow.

When choosing a fish feed, consider the following questions to determine exactly what type of fish feed you require: *Is your fish species omnivorous or carnivorous?*

This will affect the amount of protein the food needs to contain.

Is there a species-specific feed available?

Using a species-specific food will ensure optimum growth.

How large are your fish?

Mature fish can eat pellets up to 1/5 of an inch (5mm), whereas fingerlings require a smaller grade. It is possible to buy feed sized for different life-stages, or larger feeds can be crushed to suit fingerlings.

What are the feeding habits of your fish species?

Fish feed is designed to either float or to sink, in order to suit the feeding habits of different species.

Feeding fish

Use the freshest feed possible and never use feed which is damp or moldy. The amount of feed given to fish will depend on the species and the age of your stock. Fingerlings eat about 10% of their body-weight per day, and this percentage decreases as fish grow. Additionally, appetite is affected by stress and temperatures.

After estimating the amount of food needed based on species, size and number of fish, monitor your fish when eating: all of the food should be consumed within 20 minutes. If a lot is left over, this is likely to clog filters and lead to unwanted bacteria, indicating that the fish should be fed less. Most varieties of fish prefer to eat in the morning or evening, and feeding can take place up to 3 times per day.

6.5 Monitoring fish

Fish require a little more care than plants, as they are living creatures that respond quickly to any type of change in their surroundings. Monitoring of your fish is essential to keep them happy and well nourished. Let's look at what we need to check up on regularly.

Health

Fish health is dependent on environmental conditions. Therefore, monitoring pH, water temperature, ammonia and nitrites, gives a good indication of fish health. In an environment that meets their requirements, does not provoke stress and where the purity of anything added to the system is maintained, fish are unlikely to suffer from disease.

Stress levels

Stress can cause health problems and fatalities in fish. Fish are susceptible to stress caused by less than ideal environmental conditions such as those discussed previously, as well as emotional stress and stress caused by environmental changes. Stress may present as poor appetite, changes to behavior, physical injuries, aggressiveness and death.

Environmental stress can be avoided by closely monitoring ammonia and nitrite levels, ensuring adequate oxygenation and avoiding overstocking. Emotional stress can be managed by keeping the fish tank shaded and preventing sudden exposure to light and noise. Handle fish as little as possible, and do so in the dark where practical. Environmental changes on a systemic level, such as pH and temperature fluctuations, can be avoided through good system management and regular monitoring.

Harvesting

Species, as well as a range of environmental factors such as temperature, determine fish growth rates. Fish can be harvested for use at any size. Once they reach their mature size, they will also have reached sexual maturity and exhibit behavioral changes including increased aggression. Brood stock should be removed from the aquaponic unit at this time. Remaining stock should be purged for 2-3 days and harvested.

Chapter 7:

Finding plants that love those fish

Most vegetable plants are suitable for aquaponic production. The varieties which you choose will depend on your system design and environmental conditions, as well as your preferences. Plants are easily the hardiest component of an aquaponic system, and thrive in a balanced unit.

7.1 Selecting plants

Most commonly grown vegetable and herb plants will perform well in an aquaponic system. Leafy green herbs, such as lettuces, are a favorite. These plants respond well to high-nitrogen levels and low micro-nutrients, making them an excellent choice for newly established aquaponic units. They produce prolifically and quickly. Legumes and brassicas have slightly higher nutrient requirements than leafy green herbs.

Fruiting plants have more nutrient requirements again and are therefore better suited to established and well-stocked aquaponic units. They perform well in aquaponic conditions, but have more nutrient requirements than leafy greens. In particular, potassium and calcium are required for fruiting and may need to be added to the system where deficiencies are indicated.

While shallow-rooted root crops such as radish and beets can perform well in Media Beds, carrots, potatoes and other deep-rooted root crops are not suited to the system. Nor are large fruiting plants like pumpkins and melons.

7.2 Sourcing plants

Seedlings can be propagated at home or sourced from a commercial supplier. Wherever possible, plants should be raised in a soil-less medium to prevent disease and sediment from entering the system.

Seedlings can be purchased cheaply and commercially grown plants are often hardier than self-propagated ones. However, the varieties available commercially can be limited and, unless you are using a hydroponic supplier, the plants will likely be grown in a soil-based potting mix.

While it is not ideal to use plants propagated in soil, as it can contain unwanted bacteria and pathogens, they can flourish with the correct treatment. Before planting, flush the roots with water to remove all the soil particles. Once no soil is visible, briefly rinse the root system in a bleach and water mixture (1 part to 100), or another sterilizing mixture, before rinsing again in fresh water. This treatment can lead to higher levels of transplant shock in seedlings but is the only reliable method for removing unwanted soil and diseases.

It is fairly simple to propagate your own seeds in stone wool plugs or small punnets. This option is more economical than buying plants, but does require forward planning and regular watering.

7.3 Plant-friendly environments

If environmental requirements in an aquaponic system are suitable for fish and nitrifying bacteria, they will also allow plants to thrive, with only a few exceptions.

Temperature

Plants are more tolerant of ambient temperatures than the other elements of an aquaponic system. However, they do suffer when water temperatures, and therefore the temperature of their roots, becomes very warm. Lettuce, in particular, will die or bolt to seed if water temperatures top 73 degrees (23°C). Therefore, plant choice may also be influenced by the water temperature of the system as dictated by fish species.

pH level

Fluctuations in pH influence the nutrients that plants can absorb. Therefore symptoms of nutrient deficiency in plants can be indicative of a pH issue. Plants perform best in a slightly acid environment, with a pH of 6 to 7. However, the needs of bacteria and fish are more important in this regard and most plants have some tolerance of pH outside this ideal range.

Sunlight

Most vegetable plants require between 2 and 6 hours of sunlight per day. Artificial light is also acceptable.

7.4 Plant care

Plants grown in an aquaponic system tend to be fairly hardy. Monitoring the system generally and maintaining environmental conditions should prevent most problems.

Planting methods

In an NFT tube, plants which readily form water roots (leafy green herbs) can be placed directly into the cups or nets, but generally plants are grown in stone wool plugs or pellets to better support their root structure. Plugs and pellets can also be placed directly into the cups.

If using growing media, transplant your plants into the growing tray as you would a pot, gently teasing the roots out to their maximum length. Ensure that they are planted to the same depth as they were in their original containers. If plants are raised in plugs or pellets, these can be planted straight into the media.

Chapter 8:
System monitoring & maintenance

Although a well-run aquaponic system may require little actual maintenance, daily monitoring is essential. Fish and bacteria colonies are very fragile; small fluctuations in pH or even temperature can cause the destruction of the system within hours. Changes occur quickly, and plumbing malfunction can be disastrous, so the more often you can pass an eye over your system, the better. This is why it is important to put in somewhere convenient and accessible.

Good system monitoring comprises of observation as well as testing. Observational monitoring involves anecdotal evidence and the observation of fish and plant appearance and behavior, water appearance, flow volumes and even the sound of pumps and filters. Anything abnormal could be indicative of a problem, and the sooner you deal with it, the better.

Observational monitoring is a vital process. However, unless you are a seasoned grower with a very mature aquaponic system, this should not be a substitute for regular water testing. Water testing is necessary to ensure that the elements of the system are in balance, and ultimately the neglect of this key process can lead to system death if ammonia levels reach high enough proportions to cause mass fish die-off.

8.1 Water monitoring

Monitoring water qualities is one of the most important tasks undertaken in an aquaponic system. In a new system, while system cycling or when adding fish stock, monitoring of pH, ammonia and nitrates should be undertaken daily. In a more established system, testing can be reduced to once every 3-7 days, or whenever there is an indication of abnormality. Testing of water that will be added to the system is also recommended, as is testing the system whenever changes are made. It is good practice to keep a log of test results as a reference in the case of problems.

pH testing

Significant changes to pH can be an indication of systemic problems, and the changes themselves can also have an adverse effect upon system health. Additionally, it is natural for systems to become gradually acidic over time as nitric acid is a natural byproduct of the nitrification process. Therefore, it is important to monitor pH to ensure that fluctuations are minor, and to give ample time to adjust pH as necessary.

There are a variety of ways that the pH of a liquid can be tested. Most people are familiar with litmus paper and Universal Indicator, both of which are economical and easy to use. For the more dedicated grower, it may be worth investing in an electronic pH monitor.

Temperature

Temperature fluctuations can have a major impact on system health. Most growers have an electronic thermometer installed in the bio filter or fish tank. A thermometer which records daily highs and lows is particularly relevant to monitoring fish health.

Ammonia, nitrite and nitrate testing

There are a variety of testing methods which can be used to measure levels of ammonia, nitrite and nitrate in an aquaponic system. In all cases, remove a small sample of water for testing and discard after the results have been recorded.

Liquid indicator tests, which are used as per Universal Indicator, are the most reliable way to test for nitrogen compounds. Different test kits will be needed for ammonia, nitrite and nitrate, and are available from aquaponic suppliers.

Paper test strips, much like litmus paper, are also affordable but less reliable than liquid tests.

For the very dedicated grower, electronic meters are available. These are extremely accurate, but expensive. Again, a meter will be needed for each chemical being measured.

Water hardness

Water hardness should also be regularly measured. In hydroponics, Electrical Conductivity (EC) and Parts Per Million (PPM) meters, which are electronic testers, are used to measure the proportion of minerals and nutrients in a liquid. These meters are also suitable for establishing the "hardness" of a water source. However, as they do not differentiate between the types of minerals in the water, which makes them less useful for the regular monitoring of an aquaponic system.

A better option for aquaponics is purchasing liquid test kits for general hardness and carbonate hardness. As carbonates help to balance out fluctuations in pH, and are sometimes added to an aquaponic system for this purpose, it is better to use these liquid tests in order to establish an understanding of exactly what is causing your water hardness.

8.2 System adjustments

When systems are monitored regularly, major adjustments are uncommon. However, when adjustments are required, water should be manipulated in small amounts outside of the unit and added gradually wherever possible, in order to prevent fluctuations which may adversely affect fish health. The only exception to this is in the case of ammonia or nitrite toxicity, which requires immediate dilution.

pH adjustment

In the case of extremely high or low pH, additions to the water can be used to establish a balance. When adjusting pH, add the chemicals gradually, testing regularly; a small addition can cause significant changes. pH adjustment will be necessary where a water source is well outside of the ideal range. In this case, adjustments should always be made to the water before addition to the aquaponic unit. Adjustments to the unit itself are unlikely to be necessary, except to counteract gradual acidity; even in this case, changes should be made to water that is then gradually added to the system.

In the case of mildly basic water with a pH of 7-8, it is likely to reach a more ideal range once the system cycling process is complete. In extreme cases, phosphoric or nitric acid can be used to lower pH. Acidity or low pH can be raised through the addition of calcium or potassium hydroxide. In the case of the natural acidification of the system, the addition of calcium carbonate or potassium carbonate is recommended. Adding a quart (liter) of crushed egg shells, sea shells, limestone, coral or grit to the system will provide protection against pH fluctuations.

Ammonia and nitrite toxicity

If ammonia or nitrites increase above the recommended level of 0.00005 ounces per quart (1-2 mg per liter), the system requires immediate dilution. Remove 1/3 of the water and replace with fresh water before retesting. Repeat as necessary.

8.3 Regular maintenance

Beyond testing and adjustments, there is also regular maintenance required in order to ensure a functioning aquaponic system. When cleaning system parts, do so with fresh water only, as soap and cleaners may contaminate the system, killing beneficial bacteria and fish. In the case of contamination, a salt-bath can be used to sterilize materials.

Pumps

To maintain your pump, remove the filter and flush in several buckets of clean water every week. Check the fittings and flush the hoses as well.

Sediment Filters

Screens and sieves should be rinsed daily to remove accumulated solid waste. Particle filters and mechanical filters should be cleaned thoroughly each week. If media is used, treat as described below.

Fish tank

Any uneaten food or solid waste will need to be removed from the bottom of the fish tank every 3-7 days, depending on stocking density.

Bio filters

Unless it has been colonized by unwanted bacteria or algae, the bio filter and the media contained within should not be disturbed.

Growing media

The media contained in grow beds houses much nitrifying bacteria. As such, more than ¼ of the media should never be removed at any one time. That said, the media does need washing or flushing to remove accumulated salts and prevent colonization by unwanted bacteria. Clean the media by flushing well with fresh water, and scrubbing or agitating to remove any particles. Clay beads need particularly gentle handing. NFT tubes can be treated as per growing media.

Water levels

While aquaponics is a closed system, some water will be lost to evaporation and transpiration. Monitor water levels and top up the system every 7-14 days as needed, following standard procedure for additions.

Waste disposal

If discarding water from the system or from cleaning, it can go into a standard sewer or septic system. However, if diluted, this water also makes an excellent liquid fertilizer for soil-grown plants. In the case of ammonia or nitrite toxicity, extreme pH or high levels of solid waste, water can pose a hazard to the natural environment and should be diluted at a rate of 10:1 prior to disposal. Water where plant or fish disease has been identified may be a biohazard and unless a sewer system is available for disposal, authorities should be consulted.

Chapter 9:

Reeling in the success – Optimizing your aquaponic system

This chapter will give you some tips for the optimization of your aquaponic system. We will take a brief look at the plant choices per system, propagating plants, plant diversity, fish polycultures, supplementing fish feed, as well as precautionary additions for your aquaponic system.

9.1 Plant choices

One way to optimize your aquaponic system is to choose plants well-suited to your system design.

Flood and Drain

- Lettuces

- Salad greens of all types - Leafy herbs such as basil, coriander, parsley, mint and dill - Strawberries

- Water loving plants like taro, cresses, water chestnuts etc - Radishes, carrots and beets - Asian greens (bok choy etc) - Peppers and chilies - Most garden vegetables like tomatoes, cucumbers, okra, brassicas (broccoli, cabbage, etc)

NFT

Plants which form water roots: - Lettuces

- Salad greens of all types - Leafy herbs such as basil, coriander, parsley, mint and dill - Strawberries

In square-bottomed tubes with Rockwool and a training system: - Cucumbers

- Tomatoes

- Beans

Training systems usually involve overhead wires or beams, run above the growing tubes at a height of about 6 feet (2m). A piece of string is attached above and run down to each plant. Attach the string to the seedling with a loose knot and the plant will naturally climb upward. It may be necessary to tie the plants at intervals. Encourage tall plants rather than bushy ones by pinching out any side-growth.

Media Beds

Most vegetables can be grown in Media Beds, and they are particularly suited to bushy plants which do not do so well in other systems, including: - Brassicas

- Beans (bush)

- Eggplants

- Chilies

- Peppers

- Okra

9.2 Propagating your own plants

Plants for use in an aquaponic system can be easily propagated from seed. Seeds can be saved from your own crops, or purchased from certified suppliers.

Plant seeds into a soil-less growing media. Punnets filled with coconut fiber or peat work well, as do stone wool plugs. Keep the seeds moist using pure water, and when they have their second set of leaves, begin to dampen with a little water from the system or from cleaning filters, diluted at a ratio of 20:1. When the seedlings have 4 true leaves, they are ready for transplanting and the plugs can be popped straight into the growing tray or NFT tube.

Flood and Drain systems using clay beads are well-suited to propagation. Ensure that the maximum water level is 1-2 inches (2-5cm) below the surface of the growing media to avoid submerging seeds. Sprinkle seeds over the growing media and wait for germination. Alternatively, insert seeds into stone wool plugs, which can be "planted" into the growing media.

9.3 Staggered plantings and plant diversity

Planting a range of different plants will provide system security and ensure that all of the plants are not competing for the same micronutrients. Nutrient supplements are more commonly needed when systems are used to produce a plant monoculture.

Fruiting and leafy green plants can be utilized in different proportions in order to suit the amount of nutrient being produced by the system, which will in turn be affected by the stocking density of fish populations.

Staggered plantings, with roughly equal proportions of seedlings, maturing plants and plants ready to harvest, are recommended. This method better balances the amount of nutrients being drawn from the system at any given time, thus making inputs easier to calculate and preventing nutrient deficiency.

9.4 Fish polycultures

Aquaponic systems can be optimized through the use of fish polyculture, which means raising more than one type of aquatic species in the same tank. This makes better use of tank space and nutrients, depending on the specific behavioral habits of the chosen species.

Some fish are well-suited to polyculture, in particular omnivorous fish. Catfish can be raised with other fish in order to better utilize tank space. Additionally, difference species of carp can be raised together. There are many successful fish polycultures which can be used.

Additionally many aquaponic units are run as a polyculture combining fish with freshwater crustaceans or mollusks. Neither mollusks nor crustaceans produce sufficient ammonia to be the sole "fish" in an aquaponic unit. However, as scavengers, they are efficient water-filters, removing uneaten food and solid waste.

Crustaceans tend to be territorial and like to have rocks or logs to hide in or under. Ensure that any polyculture species are large enough not to become prey to one another; large crayfish will eat small fingerlings, while carnivorous fish will prey on small prawns.

9.5 Supplementing fish feed

The operating costs of an aquaponic unit can be reduced by supplementing fish feed with home-grown equivalents. In order to ensure that fish are receiving everything that they need to grow, they should still be fed at least 75% of a "complete" feed ration. The additional 25% of daily input can come from home-grown sources.

Omnivorous fish will eat plant-based supplements, whereas carnivorous fish will not. Fish intended for human consumption should never be fed animal products. Some easily produced supplemental feeds include the following types: *Aquatic plants*

Duckweed is a high protein aquatic plant that can be raised as a supplementary feed. It grows quickly and easily. However, under no circumstances should it be allowed to colonize the aquaponic unit, so only feed fish what they will eat. Other pondweeds and water plants may also make appropriate supplementary feeds.

Vegetable matter

Unwanted produce and plants can be used as a supplemental feed. Vegetable matter from your garden is only suited for some specific species. Make sure you know which fish can feed on which vegetable produce. As this depends on the fish, it is difficult to provide a quick indication here.

Live insects larvae

A variety of live insects and insect larvae are suitable feeds. Some insects which are easy and cheap to raise on a home-scale include meal worms, black soldier fly larvae and maggots.

Insect larvae should always be purged for 2-3 days before use, and should never be fed animal products if being fed to fish intended for human consumption.

Worms

Compost worms (red wrigglers, tiger worms, and others) produce prolifically and can be raised on vegetable scraps as a supplemental protein source for fish. As with insect larvae, worms should be purged before use.

9.6 Precautionary additions

One of the most common problems faced by aquaponic growers is system malfunction. Because fish and bacteria colonies are so sensitive to environmental changes, a small malfunction can result in deaths. As such, many growers take precautions to reduce the likelihood of a malfunction causing extensive damage to the system.

Some precautions which will help optimize your aquaponic system include the following: *Water storage*

If you are using water that requires treatment such as de-chlorination, or rely on electricity for your water source, keep a backup supply of water in the case of a system emergency requiring dilution or topping up. Water storage of at least 1/3 of the unit volume is recommended.

Holding tanks

An additional holding tank for fish, equipped with a pump and filter, can be a valuable resource should the system experience toxicity or temperature issues. Holding tanks can also be used for fish showing symptoms of ill-health.

Emergency shut-off

Float switches, like the ball-float valve found in a toilet, switch pumps on and off based on water levels. They can be used to prevent tanks from draining completely, or to stop them from overfilling, thus saving fish in the case of a system blockage or broken pipe. Pumps can also be fitted with shut-out valves.

Overflows

Overflow pipes connecting grow beds/sumps and fish tanks, can be used to ensure that fish tanks are not drained in the case of plumbing malfunctions.

Standpipes

A standpipe will prevent a tank from being completely drained, and are an excellent addition to both bio filter and fish tank where practical.

Alarms

Alarms can also be used to alert the grower when water levels fall or temperatures change. Additionally, some electronic meters have the potential to automatically alarm growers to system changes such as pH.

Back-up generators or batteries The health of an aquaponic system depends on pumps; without water and air pumps, water will cease to flow and oxygen levels will fall. In the case of a blackout or electrical problem, fish and bacteria can die in a matter of hours. For this reason, backup generators or batteries, in addition to extra pumps and aerators, are highly recommended. If possible, install these components to run automatically in the case of electricity outages.

9.7 Planning for system changes

It is worth noting that as fish grow, they will consume greater amounts of feed, affecting the equilibrium of the system. There are various ways to deal with this issue, including: *Under stocking*

Under stocking the system so that maximum stocking density is only reached as fish are ready for harvest will prevent severe overpopulation. However, this means that plants underperform for the majority of the growth cycle.

Altering plant proportions Under stocking can be combined with altering plant proportions so that the vegetative part of the system does not under perform in the initial stages. This means that a greater proportion of leafy herbs, requiring fewer nutrients, are grown when fish are younger, and as fish waste increases more fruiting plants are added in order to use the increase in nutrients.

Staggering populations Fish of different ages or life stages are best separated, as larger fish tend to prey on the smaller ones. However, systems can incorporate several fish tanks so that different life stages can be incorporated and a more consistent input maintained.

Chapter 10:

Troubleshooting: Fixing your fishy business

This final chapter will help you with some common troubleshooting problems, which you might encounter during your aquaponic gardening journey. Please use this chapter as a guide to solve some common problems.

10.1 Plant health: Help, my plants are sick!

Plants in an aquaponic system are less likely to suffer from diseases and deficiencies than plants in a garden. However, they can still present with the symptoms of a sickness. If just one or two plants look unhealthy, they may be diseased. However, if all of your plants look unhealthy, and particularly if this occurs more gradually, it is likely a system problem.

Deficiencies

Plants may suffer from deficiencies, normally denoted by poor growth and fruit set, or discoloration of the leaves. Deficiency is often indicative of a pH issue – it is not that the nutrients aren't there, but that the plants cannot access them. If pH is in an acceptable range, nutrient deficiencies should be treated as outlined below. Deficiencies are more common in newly established systems. Some of the most common deficiencies are: *Nitrogen deficiency*

Yellowing of leaves, beginning at the edges. Increase system input to solve this problem.

Potassium deficiency

Poor flowering and fruit set; yellow veins. Supplement with potassium hydroxide for basic systems or potassium carbonate for acidic systems.

Calcium deficiency

Poor fruit set; blossom end rot; burnt tips; leaf curl. Add calcium carbonate; add a quart (liter) of crushed egg shells, sea shells, limestone or coral to the system.

Iron deficiency

Yellow veins; leaves from yellow to white. Supplement with chelated iron to easily solve this issue.

Disease

Although more uncommon in aquaponic units than in standard gardens, plants can suffer from disease. In the case of symptoms such as fungal growths, mildews or spotting on the leaves inexplicable by deficiencies, remove and destroy all affected plants as soon as possible to prevent further contamination. Avoid planting vegetables for the same family for 6-8 months if at all possible.

Healthy plants, no fruit

Nitrogen creates lush, healthy, green leaves, and is important for plant growth. However, too much nitrogen can cause plants to produce lots of healthy foliage at the expense of flowers and fruit. If you have ruled out a potassium or calcium deficiency and have healthy looking plants, but no fruit, you may have an excess of nitrogen in the system. Dilute the system water, reduce inputs, grow leafy greens instead of fruiting plants or add more plants to the system.

If you are growing in an area where bees are uncommon, a failure to fruit could also be the result of a lack of pollination. In this case, you will need to hand-pollinate your plants to achieve fruit set.

10.2 Cleaning: Help, my growing environment is dirty!

It is important to maintain hygiene and cleanliness in aquaponic systems. A lot of sediment in the fish tank or filters may mean that you are feeding too much. If fish are consuming all food and water is still brown or cloudy, it may be necessary to install a mechanical filter or clarifier. Growing media may also be contributing to the problem if it was not well-washed before use.

Algae is an additional problem which can lead to dirty water. It grows best in anaerobic and sunny conditions. Remember to cover or shade exposed water and to use opaque containers. Ensure that water is sufficiently oxygenated and remove all algae where possible.

10.3 Fish: Help, my fish are unhappy!

Fish health is largely indicative of environmental conditions. Fish from a reputable source are unlikely to display ill-health if the environmental conditions of the system are consistent and within the recommended range. However, as disease spreads quickly, it is important to be aware of common symptoms and act quickly if illness is identified.

Signs and symptoms of disease

In addition to water testing, fish behavior and appearance should be monitored daily as an indication of overall health. Behavioral indicators of disease may include: - Increased aggression

- Listlessness

- Floating at the bottom or top of the tank, unless this is normal behavior for the species - Loss of appetite

- Rubbing or scraping the sides of the tank Physical indicators include: - Difficulty swimming

- Ulcers, lesions or discoloration on skin - Ragged fins or gills

- Decaying or moldy gills

- Swellings or growths

- Crippling

Dealing with disease

Fish that exhibit any signs or symptoms of disease should be removed from the system as quickly as possible, as should any with injuries, in order to prevent infection from spreading. Diseased fish can be treated with a salt bath. They should never be consumed.

Salt baths will kill pathogens, without harming fish. A high-concentration salt-bath can be used for 30 minutes, or fish can be placed immediately into a low-concentration salt holding tank. The procedures for moving fish should be followed, with the exception of the change from fresh to salt water. If no improvement is shown in 7-10 days, fish should be destroyed. If fish do shown improved health, a gradual reintroduction to the unit is possible.

Prevention is the best cure for fish disease. Ensure only healthy fish are added to the system, and that water, fish and food-sources are parasite and pathogen free. Good hygiene is also important – never move water between tanks, and wash or sterilize tools and materials between tanks or systems. Wash hands with soap and water before handling system materials.

10.4 System measurements: Help, my system is unbalanced!

Sometimes aquaponic systems can become unbalanced with no obvious explanation available. If you find that ammonia or pH levels are of concern and you cannot identify a cause, consider the following points: 1. Nitric acid is produced naturally in the conversion of ammonia to nitrate. Therefore, more mature systems will eventually become slightly acidic unless water has high carbonate levels, explaining the gradual lowering of pH.

2. As fish grow, they will produce more ammonia (and require more food). As such, bio filters should be sized for the maximum stocking density, not the initial fish stock.

3. Low temperatures inhibit bacteria function, and can therefore cause ammonia and nitrite toxicity as bacteria struggles to process fish waste that would be easily dealt with at higher temperatures.

Chapter 11:

Parting Words

The world of aquaponics truly shows how well nature can work together and unusual symbiosis between species can make a new ecosystem of plants and animals flourish. I truly hope that this book has provided you with some very useful information on aquaponics and everything that comes with it. Gardening in a unique way like this will give you a great new insight into what gardening can mean to you, as well as giving you some new insights into 'garden engineering' and what cool systems can help your garden become unique.

As usual, I highly recommend you only choose gardening styles and methods which will suit your lifestyle, and only consider aquaponic gardening if you are truly committed to your plants and animals, and are willing to put time and effort into it.

I hope that one day in the near future you will find yourself amongst your plants and fishes and will think of this book, and will be grateful that instead of going to the supermarket you have the absolute privilege of picking your own dinner from crops that *you* have lovingly tended.

As a closing note, I wish to thank you for taking the time to read this *Aquaponic Guide*. Through the course of this book, we have showed you the ins and outs of the possibilities of aquaponic systems. Please take the lessons from this book and apply them to the real world!

If this book was helpful to you or if you enjoyed reading this book, **please consider leaving an honest review**. This allows other readers to make an informed decision on purchasing this book. An honest review is therefore greatly appreciated. Thank you for your time and for your help, and once again for reading this book.

www.ingramcontent.com/pod-product-compliance
Lightning Source LLC
Chambersburg PA
CBHW070929080526
44589CB00013B/1443